A Kinship with Ash

A Kinship with Ash

Heather Swan

Terrapin Books

© 2020 by Heather Swan
Printed in the United States of America
All rights reserved.
No part of this book may be reproduced in any manner,
except for brief quotations embodied in critical articles
or reviews.

Terrapin Books
4 Midvale Avenue
West Caldwell, NJ 07006

www.terrapinbooks.com

ISBN: 978-1-947896-31-4
Library of Congress Control Number: 2020938182

First Edition

Cover art by Emily Arthur
Red Sky, Star Map of Home, 2014. Diptych. Screenprint on two attached sheets of dyed BFK paper. 30 x 40 inches. Unique Print.

NOTE: Several of the poems are titled with brand names of registered pesticides and herbicides: *Liberty, Calypso, Victor, Gem, Luna, Serenade,* and *Vespers*. The poet does not intend to make any claims about these specific products.

For my mother and my father

Contents

Directive												3

I

Pesticide I: Liberty										7
Heat I													8
Cows, Rain, Bees										9
Remote Sensing											10
Columbia Coal											12
Zoological Collection: Bat								13
To Softness												14
Rabbit													15
In Which I Begin to Bargain								16

II

Disintegration											19
On Lightness											21
Winter Solstice											22
Pesticide II: Calypso									23
Zoological Collection: Passenger Pigeon					24
Before Dawn												26
This World												28
Boy														29
Agoraphobia												30

III

An Incantation to Be Spoken Lakeside					33
Boy II													35
On Breaking												36
Pesticide VII: Victor									37
On Sun													38
Thaw													39
Pesticide IX: Gem										40

Mothering	41
Yellow	42
Zoological Collection: Warbler	44
And as we walked on, the ghost accompanied us from inside all the houses.	45

IV

Alchemy	49
Dear Leonard	50
Bowl	52
Another Day Filled with Sleeves of Light	53
The Curtain Maker's Children	54
Devotion	55
Relics	57
Pesticide VIII: (*Actias*) Luna	58
The Day After Summer Solstice	59

V

Empath	63
How to Love the Damaged Ones	64
And the Maple Stands Bare in the Wind	66
Heat II	67
Pesticide X: Serenade	68
One Kind of Desire	69
In February	70
What the Heart Wants in Old Age	71
Sleeping with Yaks	72
Pesticide V: Vespers	74
After	75

Acknowledgments	77
About the Author	79

I begin to believe the only sin is distance, refusal.
All others stemming from this.

—-Jane Hirshfield

Directive

   In this world of waters,
the unleashed waters,

   we wend our way
not heeding the beacons

   while the snow geese wait
for ice that never arrives

   and the swans move southward
but tarry. Who designed

   our faulty compass?
We must stop now

   and scrape the soil clear
of plastic shards and dead grass

   and with our fingernails
etch a new map

   born of bone, aware of our
kinship with ash,

   with crickets, with wrens.

Pesticide I: Liberty

for Deb

Remember how we ran through fields
of Queen Anne's lace, shirtless, our sex
still knotted like tiny fists in our chests,
jeans rolled up to the knees? And how our
ankles were crusted with mud from the creek
where we caught frogs and crawdads,
for sport, and let them go? Remember
eating ground cherries and wild raspberries,
sucking the sweet from red clover?
And the clouds of Yellow Sulfur wings
rising around us on days after rain
when they gathered on the drying puddles
in the road? And the neighbor's farm
where we raced through the halls of corn,
risking being sliced by the menacing
green knives, stealing when we were hungry,
tearing an ear open and plunging our teeth
into the firm inviting flesh? The dirt mixed
with sweat. Remember when we thought
what we should fear was the bull
we outran, and the nettles and the ticks? Before
our bodies betrayed us. Before we knew
we were doomed all along. Before we learned
of the real poisons lurking all around us.
Before I started having nightmares,
and you started carrying a gun.

Heat I

A hot wind from the west
spools through factory towers
at the edge of town, then sweeps
along the clapboard houses, rushes
down my street, thwacking screen doors
and whistling between locusts,
snapping twigs and sprinkling them
over the lines of parked cars,
touching everything.

A hot wind as thorough as pain
when it floods through a
grieving body. As inescapable
as the sound of the cello.
Birds and insects grip their branches,
and we watch from my front stoop
as it ushers in the end
of the holocene.

Cows, Rain, Bees

Once again, rain
eliminates boundaries.
Where once there was sidewalk
edged with street,
now there is only water.
In the same way, pain
can seem larger than the body,
passing through the boundaries,
emanating outward
until everything aches:
the trees, the grass,
the solitary cow
lagging behind the homeward herd,
glancing back and back
to the valley of bees.
Bees, who labor
toward a sweetness
which is taken from them
again and again,
but keep returning
from the fields of clover.

Remote Sensing

> ...This past February, for instance, Planet deployed 88 breadloaf-size satellites from an Indian Space Research Organisation rocket. They are now part of a 149-satellite constellation scanning every point on Earth several times a week.
> -Richard Conniff, *Yale Environment 360*

Here in my empty cortado glass:
a web of espresso residue
like a print of an archipelago
from the air. I think of the satellites
photographing us endlessly,
the images that show up
on my phone: the turquoise waters
escaping from the glaciers, the tangle
of the Sundarbans dancing with the sea,
the florets of flames in forests of Siberia,
the empty miles where once there were trees,
and at night, the electric blaze of our cities.
These images which invite us
to notice earth's changes, that suppose
this constant surveillance from above
will inspire us to stop the plight.
And I am moved by the pictures,
the beauty, the loss, inspired even,
to do *something* But I am so easy to distract.
In this coffee shop, I cannot even see
the horizon. Only these stucco walls,
the dark wood of this small table, and
my own unruly veins, like mangroves

sprawling across my hand, the hand
that holds this cortado glass that held
my first espresso, and I notice
how hungry I am.

Columbia Coal

Inside the factory, fine black soot
coats the floors and the walls, and soon
our nostrils and tongues. Nothing
is small in this place where coal is cooked
for power. *I've spent thirty-seven years
in here,* Jerry says, as he guides us
over steel grate bridges four hundred feet
from the ground and past the massive boilers
and dripping corroded pipes and down
to the infernal fires. He hears
and smells anything going wrong and
has risked worming his entire body
through narrow, searing tubes in order
to make repairs. I saw it was an act
of love. I thought of my mother, a potter,
also a tender of fires, who taught us to read
the colors of the flame in her kiln. She knew
when the fire was hungry and how to read
the smoke. He says they added scrubbers
to the chimneys once they knew what was
pouring out. The lines in his face are like
the map of a delta becoming more tangled
as things erode. No one told him
when he took this job he would be party
to any destruction. He just knew it was
his job to make sure lights went on
when folks flipped their switches in town.

Zoological Collection: Bat

The entire skeleton is
no taller than my palm.
Pinned to black velvet,
bones thin as pine needles,
with arms reaching wide,
away from its thimble chest
and hands with fingers
so long that, when draped
with skin, they became sails
to capture wind and propel
it upward, away from this earth
to which I'm bound.
The mastodon tooth
in the other room is the size
of my entire head.

To Softness

Is it cruelty or mercy
that after another day of horror,
the tangerine light stains the buildings,
and the silhouettes of the maple trees
on the cracked cement block walls
transform them into works of art?

And do the peach and lavender
clouds floating past mean to mock
or remind our barbaric selves?

Oh, Softness,
we have all but destroyed you
with our bullets, our bombs,
our fear.

But here: the snail, my teacher,
lifts his unarmored head
on a leaf already wet with dew
near the iris's open throat.

Rabbit

After a long numbness, I wake
and suddenly am noticing everything,
all of it piercing me with its beautiful,
radical trust: the carpenter bee tonguing
the needles of echinacea believing
in their sweetness, the exuberance
of an orange day lily unfolding itself
at the edge of the street, and the way
the moss knows the stone, and the stone
accepts its trespass, and the way the dog
on his leash turns to see if I'm holding on,
certain I know where to go. And the way
the baby rabbit––whose trembling ears
are the most delicate cups––trusts me,
because I pried the same dog's jaw
off his hips, and then allows me to feed him
clover when his back legs no longer work,
forcing me to think about forgiveness
and those I need to forgive, and to hope
I am forgiven, and that just maybe
I can forgive myself. This unstoppable,
excruciating tenderness everywhere inviting
us, always inviting. And then later, the firefly
illuminating the lantern of its body,
like us, each time we laugh.

In Which I Begin to Bargain

for my plastic bottle--the albatross
for my 4-lane--seeds unbound
for my cotton quilt--the many years of backs, the many years of hands
for my wireless--some silence
for my tortilla chips--the fields of daisies, the fields of Queen Anne's lace
for my gas cap--the polar bear, the harbor seal, the tern
for my thermostat--the mountaintops of Kentucky and West Virginia
and for my perfect lawn--frogs
for my insecticide--the songbirds' eggs, the butterflies, the bees
for my fossil fuel--the fossils, the strata undisturbed
for my palm oil--the orangutan
for my mascara--the rabbits, the mice
and for my smartphone--Congo
for my blue jeans--the seamstresses, and their eyes, their children,
    their hands
for my many myths--the crows, the bats, the rattlesnakes, the spiders
for my jet plane--the coral reef, the mollusks of many shapes
and for my mirror--skies

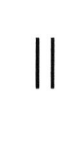

Disintegration

    1.
A voice on the radio said
   to imagine Florida was a thumb
     shrinking slowly to the size
   of a little finger.   The edges
     will change, the voice said.   The edges
     will no longer be edges.   They will be submerged
   and pulled in by the tide.
The voice suggested moving inward
   meaning farther away   from what we knew as the edge.
I imagine sitting at a cafe table   near the shore
   my hands warm around a cup of tea
     as I watch the ocean pawing its way up the beach.
   How the intricate underpinnings of the fig tree
     its lattice of dark veins
       will be washed clean of soil
     and how tables will rise and float away   white tablecloths
       undraping themselves
    until they undulate through the salt water   opaque
jellyfish.

    II.
Disintegration is fundamental. For example, the half-life of
   carbon–14 is 5730 years.
      The isotope decays, and what remains is a new element.

    III.
Over time, the inaudible brush   of enough shoes
   and the burgundy threads of the rug
     begin unbraiding themselves from the jute   fraying
   so that bits of red fiber   are swept into the air
      by the light wind of the broom.
Some rugs are for sitting on, some rugs tell stories,
      others are only for prayer.

IV.
The therapist suggests moving inward
   with a kind of attention   one gives the horizon
     when waiting for rain.
        Then redrawing your map.

V.
The voice on the radio said it will affect tourism.   It will affect ports.
   And I imagine us   in small glass-bottom boats on windless days
     going out to look down through the water   at the walls of stone,
   the useless doors with ridiculous locks.   All that we could not hold.

   And I imagine our hands   weathered by then   pressing together,
     the heat erasing the seam.

On Lightness

Outside my window,
a wren alights
on a fiddlehead fern,
and the plant is forced
to bend its green spine.
As he rests there,
the air never leaves
the bird's body--
the way he floats
through trees. And then
he takes to the sky again,
and the fern sways
upright, opening its arms,
once again, to the sun.
If only it could always
be like this:
the burden of one
never breaking another.

Winter Solstice

       At the indigo hour
I see the lilt

       of trembling light
from your candle

       raised against the quelling,
the longest night

       hollowing us
as the planet leans.

       Come to the temple
of stars, you say, and I acquiesce,

       sink to my knees,
palms open like deserts,

       as the rats sit poised
for reconnaissance

       and each seed tries
to remember its name.

Pesticide II: Calypso

> ... from καλύπτω (kalyptō), meaning
> to cover, to conceal, to hide, or to deceive

When at last he reaches
151 South, stunning corn
fields flank the road,
emerald sleeves rippling out
in every direction. In the heat
of mid-July, the corn is always
undressing––its silk undone,
its layers falling away. Each ear
like a shuttle of gold.
Untroubled by corn borers
or worms or aphids and without
a weed between the rows,
this corn is the goddess
of her landscape. Nothing
thrives here but corn.
Mesmerizing, it lures
the farmer who thinks only
of the comfort, the ease.
No real way of knowing
what enslavement lies ahead.
While small rectangular labels
at the edges of the fields
quietly reveal the poisons,
he does not pay attention
to the signs.

Zoological Collection: Passenger Pigeon

> *In 1871 their great communal nesting sites had covered 850 square miles of Wisconsin's sandy oak barrens—136 million breeding adults...Even as the pigeons' numbers crashed, there was virtually no effort to save them...*
> —John Audubon

Arranged in drawers,
the pale peach breasts
and soft gray wings
unmoving, members
of an entire species
never to be seen alive
again. Some extinctions
are collateral damage,
the curator says, while
others are the result
of lust. In days when
they flourished, hunters
shot them by the hundreds,
asphyxiated them with
burning sulfur, torched
them in their roosts. Some
even sewed shut the eyes
of live birds kept for bait:
*Put it up high, tie a string
to its foot, and when a flock
comes near, pull the string.*
Its failure to fly made
it appear to be diving down
to eat, drawing other birds in
for an easy catch.

The curator knows the date,
September 1, 1914, when
the very last one perished.
Her eyes, so wide, and birdlike
as she tells us.

Before Dawn

        The loon casts a spell
over the lake

        as the moon wanes
and earth leans back

        toward day.
Are you afraid?

        The mist lifts
like a flock

        of ghosts ascending
for some arcane

        occasion. The frogs
have not slept

        all night. Inside
the tiny house,

        the two I love
dream their secret

        dreams, and I cling
to the sweet luck

        of this life.
Are you afraid

      like I am, as it
all vanishes

      before you
like these stars

      already fading?

This World

Again: rubble, buildings ravaged
glass shattered, asphalt broken
gutters torn, fabric forgotten
upheaval, so much dust

what were living rooms
what were stairs
what were sidewalks leading to and from
what were stores to buy olives and bread
what were cafes where two could meet
what were chairs

and then the quiet after, the stumbling through
the texture of night, unfolding velvet
the rain made into columns by wind, the rinsing
the trying to find, the holding

eventually on the horizon a crease of vermillion
bright pierce, resurgence of light

somewhere a child asks questions
somewhere the table is righted
somewhere the gun is put down
somewhere a woman sees the ginkgo's radii reaching
somewhere a handful of seeds
somewhere a voice saying
   I'm sorry
   I'm so sorry
   I'm so sorry it had to be like this

Boy

He bursts from the cattails
clutching a bullfrog--
the glabrous body
slick with mud,
thick legs outstretched,
but somehow tranquil.
His hands could easily crush
this creature whose soft belly
is the color of milk,
who can breathe
through her skin,
whose only protections
are a transparent eyelid
and quickness.

This is the child who,
in the darkness, unable
to sleep, curls into
the body he came from
and asks, *But who invented war?*
And *Can a bullet go through brick?*
Can a bullet go through steel?

Now, at the water's edge,
filled with a wild holiness,
he navigates the balance,

then lets the frog go.

Agoraphobia

In the elevator she cleaves
to the proximity of contours,
the way the edge of a man's jacket
is creased so slightly by a woman
whose arm is hooked through her purse,
and how their scents compress:
coffee, wood smoke, sandalwood, sweat.
She takes hallways to avoid
the centrifuge of the atrium,
making her way to the little room
filled with the paintings of Van Gogh.
The press of each brushstroke
against the next makes
even the expanse of a wheat field
seem incapable of swallowing.
She has seen how a grain of salt
disappears in a glass of water.
How even the perfect container
of the tulip falls away.
So most days she writes letters
she'll never send to anyone,
just to tuck them
into an envelope's embrace.

An Incantation to Be Spoken Lakeside

after Thompson's Algae Bloom on Fish Lake

the way it defies gravity
always invisibly rising
the way its white breath floats high above
the way it holds the sky up to itself
reflecting the light the blue
and the way it doubles
the birds passing through
the way it trembles at the wind's caress
the way it always responds
the way it circles our oars, our limbs
the embrace of the unconditional
the way it allows the bodies of fish
the bodies of frogs the tiny
blue-green algae bodies
the way it offers itself to the thirsty
and takes whatever comes
the way it reflects our faces
reflects the things we love
the love we have for perfect lawns
the perfect green of perfect lawns
the phosphorus we pour and pour
the way it opens to whatever comes
to what comes pouring off our streets
the way it swallows whatever comes
and the swirl of green grows and grows
a floating raft of poison
the way it does not protest even while it's choking
the way it does not discriminate or warn
the way it still offers itself to the mouths
of the animals who come in darkness

not knowing how toxic the green
the deadly perfect lawn green
the way it will hold the bodies of dogs
and the bodies of cows when they weaken
and when they begin to twitch
and when they begin to stiffen
and the way it will carry them after

Boy II

The Green Darner unzips
the air above the cattails
and the sparrow threads
the trees with song,
unspooling sounds
that make this landscape
our known one. The smell of
Queen Anne's lace and
juniper on our pant legs,
the softness of a leopard frog's
belly and the weight
of honeybee footsteps
on our hands--
all making a kind of home
for you, for me.
It is to these I turn
when you turn from me
and run--bridle off--
at full gallop into a new field
you will soon know well enough
to call your own.

On Breaking

Those early days, when you were
small enough to carry,
my entire life curved
like a nautilus around you.
You were separate,
but not severed.

Never have I been so raw, child,
as I felt bringing you into this world
of both violets and beheadings.

How can we remain open?
What choice do we have
but to don our armor
in order to go forth each day?

But to be most alive
we must be willing
to be broken, over and over,
to keep our palms open,
those muscles in our chests
unbarbed, in whatever body
we're given.

So may you open like the orchid,
my child, I beseech you.
The wind blows, the leaves fall.
There is no compass but love.

Pesticide VII: Victor

The handfuls of dead bees
she finds after the spraying
are not the worst part
for the beekeeper.
It's the bees still struggling
that gets to her. Limping
in a circle like someone
who's been spinning
on a tire swing for too long,
who then stands--dizzy,
nauseous, stunned.
Their wings shudder,
but they cannot fly.
These insects whose bodies
know the rhythm
of the blossoms,
the changing angles
of the sun, whose alchemy
gives us liquid gold,
whose love affairs
with pistils and stamens
give us apricots,
almonds, melons.
To witness is to be
dredged, she thinks.
What war do we think
we're winning?

On Sun

shattered by gray clouds

bringing into focus again

the gray moraine, the lake

of gray. Not the apocalypse

but the partial eclipse of the heart-

land, midwinter. Encryptions

you left, like fractures in the ice

now covered in drifts, persist.

Then the wind lifts the snow,

like a million granules of sand,

and for the time it takes me

to gasp at your ghost again,

the air a rage of stars.

Thaw

Not love, but fire
built against the bitter cold.
The solitary woman,
and the solitary man
peel something tender.
What does our skin know
of itself except what
presses against it?
Cheek brushing sternum,
forearm brushing breast,
then fingers, lips--all
the necessary tinder.

Pesticide IX: Gem

It's not a dwelling they're building,
he said, about the bowers of the bower
birds. They scavenge the best detritus,
whatever gems they can find–
a leaf, a berry, a shell, a feather,
bits of plastic or broken glass--
in monochromatic hues, and then
in an array of cerulean or tangerine
or russet or bone or black,
they build their temples to longing.
It's not a dwelling at all, he said.
It's like a story waiting to be read.

Mothering

Seven grackles, blueing in the light,
marshal our movements as we scurry below
the boiling sky while the city sirens warn us
of tornados. Clouds the color of tempered steel
muscle toward your house on the hill
as branches of the maple flail in revery
or in terror. You shine at moments like this.
You've swept through the house
gathering blankets and candles, secured
them in the basement. You have two radios
sputtering out facts, and your eyes gleam
with preparation. We shelter my daughter
and the dog, but we don't go down to safety.
Instead we stand on the porch to watch,
wind whipping our hair. I remind you
of when you made cinnamon toast, hot
chocolate, and a nest of pillows on the porch
so my sister and I could watch the storms
approach when we were kids. You tell me
you and my aunt would run the ocean's
edge when hurricanes were coming and wait
until the rain splattered your faces
before running as fast as bodies can
the several blocks back home. You, who
jumped out of airplanes after your perilous father
forbade it. You, whom my father left, and whose
second marriage was to a madman. You point
to the menacing cumulus and laugh.

Yellow

    I.
Chamomile-steeped afternoon,
and she stands at the window
as if light had hands capable of holding.
Outside, September unbuttons
the landscape of shyness.
Something pierces--
as a lemon opened
can pierce the air.
Something like a face
appearing at the door
after a long silence.

    II.
As yolks in seamless shells,
they blindly became themselves.

    III.
Back then, in early light
the man would pull the small boy from the damp sheets,
the boy who, struggling against sleep,
moved like an animal just born,
then stumbled with the shove toward the bath.
All ears crouched, knowing what came
with stripping of sheets. If only
she had thought to rise before
and substitute dry things,
but she, too, was a child,
so instead she had closed
her door.

    IV.
Even in the driest summers,
corn stalks rose
from the ground.

    V.
Now in the late angle
of the sun, bees move
with steady attention,
bodies knowing
the meaning of winter.
No use measuring
how long sweetness lasts.
Today, the radiance of mums.

Zoological Collection: Warbler

She has turned the bird inside out
separating its skin from its flesh,
the skin unzipped along the belly
then lifted like a nightgown
and gathered at the throat,
but still attached to the skull.
She can right it quickly for us,
as we gather around her in the lab.
The skin still holds its gray flight
feathers and the lighter softer
feathers underneath. Flight feathers
which, when normally arranged,
were designed to navigate branches
and dive through pools of air,
now so disheveled and tangled,
it seems to have suffered some terrible
fight. Its small body, the deep red
of not-quite-ripe plums, all that made
it move––its muscles, its lungs,
its heart––all of this
will be burned. I can't bear
to look at its eyes. Later, she
will fill its body with cotton
and stitch it closed again, store it
in the proper drawer. Visitors
like us will come to see its body,
visually pleasing by then, any
violence carefully masked.

And as we walked on, the ghost accompanied us from inside all the houses.

—Walter Benjamin

Once I saw a painting
of a skeleton filled
with sentences,
each bone a poem,
a fragment of a life.
Today I wake alone,
boil water,
pour it over
the coffee grounds.
A bird leaves the tree.
I pull on my jeans
and shoes. In winter,
you held your cup
in both hands,
your face erased by steam.
Some things are etched
into the body itself,
still your ghost presiding.

IV

Alchemy

Bubbles rise from the sea floor
like hundreds of silver balloons
in a gray room at some macabre
celebration. An exhortation.
Coral fans–the color of concrete,
the color of winter, or midnight–
gesture with their graying fingers.
A memorial, an omen.
Red sky in the morning, sailor take warning.
Gray ocean floor, the closing of a door.
We swim through the tomb
logging legacies of extinction,
regret big as the body of the whale,
beached, with breath receding.
Speed boats churn above.
We witness, here, our alchemy.
Carbonic-acid swells crest and crash,
leach into water-born babies,
and the shells of crabs soften
and soften. Each of us knows
the recipe for poison. On the dock,
a perch is held captive: a rarity,
a specimen, a symptom. His body
seizes in its final arcs. Then, only
his eye tips wildly, like a tin plate
hung in the wind by the garden
to scare something nefarious away.

Dear Leonard

I needed a roof
        in the pouring rain

and you were steel
        while one storm

chased another,
        wind blowing

whole buildings
        down. You were

roof and railing,
        base note

and holy ghost.
        You held

my shaking shoulders
        as we walked

over the wet ground
        to where, on my knees,

I pushed bulbs
        into soil,

not knowing the way mud
        holds the boot first

before dragging
        the whole body down.

Bowl

for my mother

From the mud in her hands,
the bowl was born.
Opening like a flower
in an arch of petals,
it became a vessel
both empty and full.

Later, in the kiln
it was ravaged by fire,
its surface etched and vitrified,
searing the glaze into glass
as its body turned
to stone.

It is at the edge of damage
that beauty is honed.
And in Japan,
the potter tells me,
when a tea bowl
cracks in the fire,
that crack is filled
with gold.

Another Day Filled with Sleeves of Light

and I carry ripened plums,
waiting to find the one
who is interested in tasting.

How can we ever be known?

Today the lily sends up
a fifth white-tipped tendril, the promise
of another flower opening,
and I think, this must mean this plant
is happy, here, in this house, by this window.

The taller plant leans and leans toward the light.
I turn it away, and soon its big hands are reaching again
toward what nourishes it,
but that it can never touch.

Couldn't the yellowing leaves of the maple
and their falling also be a sign of joy?
Another kind of leaning into.
A letting go of one thing
to fall into another.
A kind of trust I cannot imagine.

The Curtain Maker's Children

We learned early when the needle slips
and punctures the tip of your finger
to press the thumb against the wound
to hold the pain and the liquid in
until it's numb enough to continue
with no evidence, no mess.
All the fabric was passed down to us,
and we knew the patterns well--
how to make the heavy drapes of crepe
to draw against the world, to keep it
from peering in at any unspeakable thing:
a man whipping his wife with wet towels
as she sits tied to a chair, her cupboards
empty, her arms growing thin.
And each of us received a quilt, with our names
sewn in. We learned how to make our beds,
how to stitch a perfect seam, and
even when to open the windows
so the sheers could harbor air.

Devotion

for R.W.

Tracking coyote at 3 a.m.
in the wind of a Wyoming winter,
she stood in the bed of the pickup
sweeping the antennae along the horizon
for signals the collars made.
Gloves were too clumsy
for the necessary quickness,
and her hands grew so cold,
they seemed to separate
from her body.

The animals moved as secretly as blood,
and the signals came in a shower of beats,
dancing off the mountains. Pinpointing
their source was as difficult as trying
to locate the heart in the body, with touch
your only guide—first a throbbing in the neck,
now the temple, now the wrist.

For fourteen months she followed them.
She washed their scat in white cotton bags
and discovered the stuff of medicine bundles:
bird bones, rabbit claws, mice teeth.
Once she looked one in the eye.
There was no trace of recognition.

Today she steers my canoe.
The creases we leave in the water's surface
soon disappear

like lines on the face of a child.
Trees whisk a cup of blue.
Insects and frogs, antiphonal.

We struggle to name the birds:
kingfisher, cormorant, wren,
and then laugh at the need to name them.
She confesses sometimes she hears ghosts at night
and laments love's hollow corridors.
And when I read to her the Neruda ode,
in which he rescues a bee from a web,
she tells me she feels sad for the spider
who's left hungry after so much work.

Relics

> *Because of the grace remaining...they were
> an inestimable treasure for the holy congregation.*
> —metmuseum.org

They kept the toenail of the Saint
in the shrine room, incense
tempering the air. Tiny tombs
with gold foil fans edged
in sapphire stones. And so much
stained glass, flare. Lips of monastics
have whispered prayers that linger
in the swing of silk robes
as temple dwellers patrol
the sacred. I long to belong,
to taste the truth they taste. I'll bow,
I'll bring my forehead down. I'll lay
my sinner's body down. I'll tell it
straight: faith failed to find
its footing in me when the bodies
continued to fall, the conqueror's
goblets filled and filling,
filled and spilling out. Tell me
Saint, what must we do? Tell me
which prayer is the right one?

Pesticide VIII: (*Actias*) Luna

At the blue hour
in the firefly forest
with nightjars thrumming
the darker shades down
and stars slowly waking--
the silk of June air brushes
her shoulders, loosens all
that was bound. The woman
stands barefoot on the worn
wooden stair, fearing nothing,
at last. Feeling, for once,
whole. The coyotes begin
their chatter as night
continues to fold. Then
she turns and swoons
at the pale traveller
resting in the lamplight,
fragile as a paper kite,
but capable of flying
for miles.

The Day After Summer Solstice

for D

  We were awash in chords of light,
mourning doves providing a foothold,

  and all that was lost--from the turquoise
earrings and old loves to friends

  with cancer and conversations
fading with the years--pressed in.

  But the light breeze reminded our skin,
saying *here*, saying *this*,

  and steadied us, gave us ballast
out of which grows the determined

  and tremulous gaze
that love requires.

V

Empath

> *We have to consciously study how to be tender*
> *with each other until it becomes a habit...*
> —Audre Lorde

The pistols glinted in the moonlight
pouring through the trees by the bike path
as two men robbed my son and his friend.
One gun pressed into his friend's temple
as he lay face-down on the ground;
the other pointed at my son's chest. He obeyed:
slipped off his backpack, emptied
his pockets, handed the taller man his chapstick
and his phone, which, minutes before,
had sent the message, *On my way,* to me.
He knelt down and turned his back when asked,
as one might before uttering a prayer,
the universal gesture of supplication.
In the grass, damp with dew, he prepared
for the closing of night, the silencing
of tree frogs, but the gunshot never
arrived. Instead the men ordered them
to run away, and so they ran, hearts glad
to be pounding louder than their footsteps
like bass drums at some celebratory parade,
all the way home. Later, telling the story,
he says he imagined as he ran the desperation
of those men—*Not much older than me!*—
that pushed them into a life like that.
Like a rabbit looking up at the hawk
and not seeing talon or beak,
but the soft underside of the wing.

How to Love the Damaged Ones

      See how the body of the horse
flinches when she startles?

      How her flesh flickers,
haunch rippling like soil in a quake,

      hooves pawing the ground as if
trying to move backward in time,

      eyes wide, neck arching back
to see more

      of what might
bite or bruise her?

      Not because you mean
to harm her,

      but memory drives
her reflexes

      and adrenaline spikes
clutch the brain.

      Don't give up.
Lean in.

      Only when your hand
and your voice become

        as common as breath,
and as kind,

        will her heartbeat slow,
her face soften,

        and you will be surprised
by how far she can run

        and what she'll be willing
to carry.

And the Maple Stands Bare in the Wind

No, not the kind of exposure
that leaves you feeling closer
to anything. The other kind.
Like fingers bared
in frigid air.

The fox
bounds through the snow
as though it's a field of clover and crabgrass.
The chickadees
return and return, in this cold,
the skin of their feet
not cracking,
their wings still capable of flight.

How is it we were not built
to endure but rather
to grow numb in the cold,
to slowly cease to function?
Your silence colder
than any winter wind.

These are seeds, I keep telling myself,
about the stalks and heads
of dead flowers
vamping like mannequins
over the drifts.

Heat II

Tiny goblets of light
        cling to branches at dawn
and the meadow shimmers
        with hoarfrost diamonds
as my dog and I make our way
        east. The cold finally bites my skin
after too many weeks
        of rain. Unseasonably hot,
ice skates idle by the door.
        Meanwhile, Australia burns on TV
on the other side of this world.
        In a photograph, a farmer
cradles his lamb, limp and unbreathing
        in his arms. No one can warn
the animals. And the fires rage on
        just out of the frame.

Pesticide X: Serenade

after the recordings of Bernie Krause

The clatter of leaves, the wind's rich bass,
the tremolo of water, and the rasp of soil shifting
as worms worked their way through.
In the beginning, he recorded the sounds for pleasure.
The symphonies of the forests, the prairies, the bogs.
The harmonies of frogs, monkeys, birds.
The years passed, and the spaces grew quiet. One by one
the voices were silenced. Now he records
the absence, all that we've undone.

One Kind of Desire

Fevered head on a pillow,
lids closed on a mind
capable of drawing a woman
in a tower leaning out
from a small window
to paint a bird on the sky.
Or a mermaid calling
from the cold blue ocean
to a lion made of stars.
Once, only a tangle of wires
tethered you to this world.
They had cut me to take you
out of my body. I had a choice
then, to continue leaning
toward you, or turn away.
Love is a cliff in high wind
with no handholds. I chose
to lean toward, by some miracle
and here we are now, you
dreaming your fevered dreams,
me holding the cold cloth
on your forehead, praying
you'll paint another sky.

In February

Sunlight spills across the room,
sharpening the leaves
of the oxalis, turning dust
to luster, pulling the
shadows long. Light the
color of the honey we pulled,
poured straight from the comb,
then licked from each other's hands.
The outside is always slipping in,
the way your gaze enters me
again, spills and spreads, and changes
everything. Everything.

What the Heart Wants in Old Age

When I dream of us, I dream of animals

on a mountain lying beneath a night sky

with nothing between breath and starlight,

pulse and wind, but the sounds of ice melt

and pine bough meeting other.

I wake craving something deep and old

like stone or spring water, wanting

to go in unfettered, to taste something true

with you, to taste its honey, its salt,

and anchor there for a time, to be

traversed by it and known

like the soil is known by tree roots--

something that requires

shedding everything but mercy.

Sleeping with Yaks

After climbing through rhododendron
forests, over dizzying gorges on bridges
made of rope, through villages where women
made paper out of bark next to Himalayan
ice melt, past tiny stone stupas and
countless fluttering prayer flags to where
the snow began and trees no longer grew,
I came, at dusk, to a two-room home.
A family of sherpas ushered me inside,
handed me a bowl of boiled potatoes
and a cup of hot butter tea, then invited me
to stay the night. And after sitting
in the glow of the fire, my body melting
in the holy silence, the woman led me
to an adjacent room where the family
kept their yaks--a room not much larger
than their two enormous bodies--
and she shook out a mat on the floor
near their heads which were easily wider
than my chest. Each of their ears
was adorned with a pompom made of yarn
the red of valentines. The woman and I
bowed goodnight to each other,
and I was left alone with the yaks.
We measured each other with our eyes.
I blinked mine slowly in a kind deference
and waited for them to blink back,
then I folded myself down in the narrow space
between the wall and their faces,
and rolled out my blanket

under their whiskery chins. All night,
as the cold mountain shifted under the stars,
they held me in the warm halo
of their sweet, even breath.

Pesticide V: Vespers

By the lake's edge at dusk,
a raft of lavender ice
is being consumed by
the warming blue.
Seagulls reel and vie
for what is vanishing
months too soon.
Redwing blackbirds
clamor for the foreground
as a train whistle spools
through town--the boxcars
heaped with coal.
The factory hums on,
its wires reliably pulsing
so we can endlessly
use our phones.
A greyhound bus roars
along a bank of trees,
and two long boats
scissor the water below,
scullers thrusting
to the shouts
of the coxswain,
embodying the churn
of forward motion
humans seem
to love. But here,
on a mat of branches
and sand, quiet as monastics
in a chapel, two cranes
stand perfectly still.

After

     There among the silences
find the ghost tree--

     the split black branches making
fissures in the clearing.

     Watch as the fog dresses
and undresses the wounds,

     the suppuration of bark,
so raw underneath.

     The birds can find
no purchase.

     Scavenge the esker,
make a circle of stones,

     kneel down wreathed in
feather and bracken.

     Prepare to knit yourself
back into the world.

Acknowledgments

I am grateful to the following publications in which some of the poems first appeared:

About Place Journal: "Columbia Coal," "Victor"

Basalt: "On Sun," "Agoraphobia," "In Which I Begin to Bargain"

Edge Effects: "Incantation to Be Spoken Lakeside"

Cold Mountain Review: "Sleeping with Yaks"

Comstock Review: "Devotion"

Green Humanities Review: "Another Day Filled with Sleeves of Light"

The Hopper: "After," "Pesticide V: Vespers," "Pesticide IX: Gem"

Midwestern Gothic: "Pesticide I: Liberty"

Phoebe: "Untitled VII"

Poet Lore: "The Curtain Maker's Children"

The Raleigh Review: "Thaw "

Wildness: "In February"

"Empath" was published in *Healing the Divide: Poems of Kindsness and Connection,* ed. James Crews (Green Writers Press, 2019).

"Pesticide II: Calypso" was published in *becoming-Botanical,* eds. Josh Armstrong, Alexandra Lakind, and Chessa Adsit-Morris (Objet-a Creative Studio, 2019).

"Pesticide I: Liberty" was reprinted in *New Poetry from the Midwest 2019*, ed. Rita Mae Reese and Hannah Stephenson (New American Press, 2020).

"In Which I Begin to Bargain" and "Victor" were reprinted in *Rewilding: Poems for the Environment,* ed. Crystal S. Gibbons (Split Rock Press, 2020).

I am also grateful to the University of Wisconsin Departments of English and Creative Writing, the Nelson Institute's Center for Culture History and the Environment, University of Wisconsin Trout Lake Limnology Station's Writer-in-Residence Program, and the Sitka Center for Art and Ecology for their support.

These poems would not have come into the world without the inspiration, wisdom, and scaffolding provided by Jane Hirshfield, Laurie Sheck, Ron Wallace, Jesse Lee Kercheval, Amaud Jamaul Johnson, James Crews, Stella Nelson, David Zimmerman, Cherene Sherrard, Mary Fiorenza, Ron Harris, Spring Sherrod, Julie Palmer, Brenda Weiss, Andrew Mahlstedt, Ian and Jennifer Boyden, Nathan Jandl, Spencer Maughan, Daegan Miller, Jake Kosek, Jenny Conrad, David Axelrod, Nancy Judd, Deb Sullivan, Jeanie Garvey, Marc Basch, Anna Waters, and my patient and insightful editor, Diane Lockward. I owe so much to the painter Arthur Kdav who helped me learn to look deeply and to the potter Stephanie O'Shaughnessy who taught me how to navigate difficulty with beauty and laughter. I am so grateful to my brilliant children, Elijah and Maia, for their love and vital humor, and to Drew Szabo for the anchor he provides.

About the Author

Heather Swan is a poet, nonfiction writer, and teacher. Her chapbook *The Edge of Damage* won the Wisconsin Fellowship of Poets Award. Her poetry has appeared in journals such as *Poet Lore, Cold Mountain Review, Phoebe, The Raleigh Review*, and *Midwestern Gothic*. Her nonfiction has appeared in *Aeon, Belt Magazine, Catapult, Edge Effects, ISLE*, and *Minding Nature*, and her book *Where Honeybees Thrive: Stories from the Field* won the Sigurd F. Olson Nature Writing Award. She has been the recipient of an Illinois Arts Council Poetry Fellowship Award, the Martha Meier Renk Fellowship, and the August Derleth Award for Poetry. She teaches writing and environmental literature at the University of Wisconsin-Madison, and she is also a beekeeper. This is her debut full-length collection.

www.heatherswan.net